BAD BE

A guide to the effe... ...nd discipline

Other books in the series:

Tantrums and Tempers
Fighting, Teasing and Bullying
Worries and Fears

BAD BEHAVIOUR

How to deal with naughtiness and disobedience and still show you love and care for your child

Dr John Pearce

THORSONS PUBLISHING GROUP

First published in 1989

British Library Cataloguing in Publication Data

Pearce, John, 1940 Oct. 27–
Bad Behaviour : how to deal with naughtiness and disobedience
1. Children. Behaviour modification
I. Title II. Series
649'.64

ISBN 0-7225-1723-8

Illustrations by *Willow*

To Rachel, Clare and Anna

Published by Thorsons Publishers Limited, Wellingborough, Northamptonshire NN8 2RQ, England

Printed in Great Britain by Cox & Wyman, Reading, Berkshire

1   3   5   7   9   10   8   6   4   2

CONTENTS

INTRODUCTION

Everyone knows that difficult and disobedient behaviour is part of normal child development, but that doesn't make it any easier to deal with. In fact one of the most frequent arguments between parents is over what they should do when their child has been naughty. Difficult children also cause disagreements and tension between family friends and relatives as well as between teachers and parents. The result of all this is that having a badly behaved child becomes a frequent cause of shame, embarrassment and even danger for parents.

There is a frequent problem that parents face: which of the many approaches to discipline should they adopt? How are they going to decide which method works the best? Of course what usually happens is that one method is tried and if that does not work, then another is attempted, and another. . . and another. In the end any parent will be inclined to give up or give in, leaving a child who is confused about what is expected.

A lot of bad behaviour is simply due to children not knowing what is right and what is wrong, rather than to any wish to be difficult and disruptive. They have not yet been taught (disciplined) to do the right thing, so they copy what they see around them. Unfortunately, bad behaviour often seems to get the desired results quicker than being good, and there is no shortage of examples of bad or naughty behaviour for children to copy.

The different methods of discipline covered by the book

BUT THERE'S ONLY *ONE* LEFT . . . . . .   OH, BETTER LET *HER* HAVE IT TO KEEP HER *QUIET* . . . .

BAD BEHAVIOUR OFTEN SEEMS TO GET THE **DESIRED RESULTS** QUICKER . . .

are based on methods which have been well researched and found to be effective. . . even in the most difficult children!

But this book is not particularly about difficult or disturbed children. It is about normal children and day to day problems which are not a major concern, but nevertheless take up your time and energy and can even build up into a big problem if allowed to continue.

You may think that I take a rather firm line that could cause children to become upset, but if you read the book carefully you will find there is always a good reason for being tough. Love and indulgence are not the same thing; indeed, more trouble is caused by parents giving in 'for a quiet life' than by anything else. It is not easy to stick to what you have said, especially if you are not sure that you are doing the right thing in the first place.

I would like you to feel that I am talking directly to you as you read through the book. You can 'talk' back to me if you don't agree with what I am saying or if you don't understand. Then read on and it should become clear why I have taken a certain line rather than any other. Don't hold back from having an argument with me in your head or asking someone else what they think. In this way you will become much clearer about what you believe yourself.

Do remember that if I recommend a particular way of

dealing with a problem that seems to be very tough and potentially upsetting for the child, this is because I know it is effective and does no harm to a child. Young children need firmness and structure in their lives in order to give them a feeling of security. In fact, being tough and firm in setting limits on children's behaviour is one way of showing them that you love and care for them.

If you are unsure about your own ideas, I would like you to follow my suggestions as closely as possible, in spite of any reservations you might have. I have been very careful to give guidelines and advice only where I am confident that it is safe, reasonable and effective. If you have followed the guidelines and they have not worked, please don't immediately think that I have got it all wrong. It is perhaps more likely that you are not sticking closely enough to what I have said. Read it again, have another go and don't give up!

CHAPTER 1

UNDERSTANDING DISCIPLINE

It is a shame that the word discipline is often used in a negative and authoritarian way. The word comes from the Latin—*disciplina*—meaning teaching, which is both positive and constructive. Unfortunately, many people think of discipline as meaning punishment and being very strict, so they try and avoid using the word. Although there is no proof, it does seem as though the less people talk about discipline the more badly behaved children become and the more other possible causes are thought about, such as:

- food additives
- too much television
- both parents out working
- a breakdown of traditional values in society
- single parent families
- poverty and unemployment.

In some individual cases there may be some evidence to support the causes listed above, but it would be wrong to generalize and say that nowadays all children are naughty and undisciplined. Indeed, a few children are very well behaved. Nevertheless there are many pressures in our everyday life that make it difficult to provide the time and care that children need, but don't feel despondent, there is a lot that you can do to make sure that your child is reasonably obedient and isn't a pain in the neck.

The poor outlook for difficult and disobedient children

means that it is no good sitting around hoping that they will grow out of it—many of them won't. In fact, the longer a child goes on misbehaving, the longer the problems are likely to persist in the future. Most naughty children under the age of 5 grow out of it and become reasonably well behaved, but badly behaved children over 5 years old have a strong tendency to continue being difficult, disobedient and possibly delinquent. So, if you would like your child to be reasonably well behaved, you will have to start your discipline early on!

Spoiling

If babies and young children were reasonable creatures who understood that other people have needs as well, there would not be much of a problem. You could respond to their every need and they would stop being difficult and demanding just as soon as their needs were satisfied. Unfortunately babies are not born reasonable and they have to be taught that other people have needs too. Until children have learnt this lesson they tend to work on the principle of 'the more you get, the more you want'.

You can see that if you continue to give in to every want, you will end up with a child who is very demanding and doesn't take other people's needs into consideration, in short, a spoilt brat. You might imagine that it would be nice to be spoilt, but in reality it leads to a great deal of distress for the spoilt child, not to mention the parents. Why else do you think spoilt children whine, moan and cry so much? This is an important point, because it means that at some stage parents will have to stop satisfying their child's every need if they want to avoid their baby growing up into a spoilt young person.

Saying 'no'

Looking after a new baby is so exciting and time-consuming that it takes most parents ages before they realize that they should be saying 'no' sometimes. Many parents leave it until their child's demands have become excessive and difficult (if not impossible) to meet. For some parents this stage will be after a few months, but for other parents it may take several years before they realize that they have a little monster who is impossible to satisfy. By this time the child will be so skilled at being demanding and manipulative that it won't be easy to change things without a lot of hard work and some distress for everyone concerned.

Perhaps the best time to start saying 'no' is as soon as you feel that your child is being unreasonable. But how can you tell what is unreasonable? Here are some ideas to help you:

- the baby stops crying as soon as you pick it up
- the crying is not that of an ill child, and there are no other signs of illness
- the baby always cries at the same time of day (or night)
- giving any attention at all immediately stops the difficult behaviour
- the crying or problem behaviour starts again as soon as your attention is withdrawn, even though the child is well and has toys to play with.

You can see that even tiny babies can be unreasonable at times, so it is a good plan to start saying 'no' at a very early stage. In this way you can gradually introduce your child to the idea that there is a limit to how many needs can be met, and your child will gradually come to know the limits of what is acceptable and what is not. This is what discipline is all about.

It is worth while remembering that there are many ways of saying 'no', some of which are outlined on the following page.

THERE ARE MANY WAYS OF SAYING NO....

- with a sharp tone of voice
- giving a loud shout
- saying 'no' in a whisper
- shaking your finger
- frowning and making a cross face
- turning away and giving no attention.

Saying 'yes'

You might think that all parents have to do is to be good at saying 'no' and their child will become well behaved, but this is not so. All that happens if you say 'no' frequently enough is that your child stops behaviour of any type and becomes inhibited. By being good at saying 'no' you will be able to stop much of your child's bad behaviour so at first it may seem as though you have a very good child. However, children also need to be told what they can do as well as what they are not allowed to do.

In theory it should be possible to say 'yes' and give praise every time a child does something good and as a result it would never be necessary to say 'no'. This is an interesting idea, but in practice it could never work because there are so many dangerous situations in our everyday life. The dangers of fire, water, electricity and roads have to be taught at an early age and it is much easier to say 'don't. . .' rather than 'do. . .'. However, it is very important to teach children about danger in a positive way as well as using negative words such as 'no' and 'don't'.

By using a positive approach to discipline and training,

you will have much more effect on how your child copes with danger. However, discipline is not only necessary to protect a child from harm, it is also needed for the child to fit in and to become a useful member of society.

Love and indulgence

We often think of love not just as a feeling of affection and caring, but also as an act of giving and self-sacrifice. Certainly this is what parents need to do for their children: they have to give up something of themselves if the love that they have for their child is to have any lasting effect. Loving and giving are so closely related that parents sometimes show their love by being indulgent and giving in to their child's demands, or by giving extra toys or food.

IT IS SO MUCH EASIER TO GIVE TOYS AND FOOD RATHER THAN **TIME AND ATTENTION**....

It is so much easier to be indulgent and to give toys and food, rather than giving up something of yourself, but children need your time and attention, your supervision and your protection—how difficult it is to be a parent! If you are too indulgent and give, for example, too many toys, your child will become more difficult and demanding. If on the other hand, you sacrifice your own needs too much, the child will become overdependent and family relationships will become tense and difficult. So indulgence has a negative and potentially harmful side as well as a positive, caring side, and parents have to keep the balance between being too indulgent and too self-sacrificing.

Here are some situations to watch out for, where it is especially easy to get the balance wrong and show your love for your child by being overindulgent or by giving up too many of your own needs.

- When your child is ill, it is necessary to be more loving and indulgent, but it can be overdone and it can be difficult to get back to normal when the child is better. In chronic or life-threatening illness it is particularly difficult to get the balance right.
- If one parent is rather strict, the other one will want to be more soft and indulgent to compensate for this.
- Youngest or only children, and of course first-born children, are often given extra love and attention which can easily involve indulgence or self-sacrifice.
- Divorced or separated parents will normally wish to show their children that they still love them in spite of all the sadness and distress that has occurred and this often takes the form of overindulgence.
- Parents who have had a deprived or difficult childhood are likely to give too much to their children because they have missed out themselves.
- Grandparents sometimes encourage parents to be overindulgent and give too much to their children.
- Some parents are soft and indulgent by nature and set themselves up to play the role of a martyr. If this is the case this role will be played in every aspect of the parents' life and not only when with their children.
- Parents who are ill or distressed will tend to give in easily, partly to make life easier, but partly because they feel guilty that they are not able to give enough of themselves to the child.

- Feelings of guilt are a common reason for parents being overindulgent and giving in easily. This happens quite frequently when parents have to spend extra time away from their children, for example, if they work full-time.

Most of us will recognize something familiar in these situations and this is why we all find it difficult to get the balance right; the balance between loving without over-indulgence and caring without smothering.

Starting at the beginning

It doesn't take long for a new-born baby to do something that is unwanted and upsetting for the parents. It may only be crying when there is nothing obviously wrong or not taking the feed properly. At this young age we usually make allowances and think up all sorts of reasons why the baby might be difficult, such as:

- is it 'wind'?
- could she be teething?
- I think he must be hungry
- she might be overtired
- you can see he is in pain
- she doesn't like being alone
- he wants a cuddle
- she must be allergic to the milk
- he is just like his father, always making a noise!

It takes most parents quite a while to realize that some-times their baby can be difficult for no more serious reason than that it is bored and wants to see some action. Even so, many parents do not see their baby as being unreasonable in its demands and they continue to make excuses for many years.

So when is it that children first become 'difficult' and start to manipulate other people in order to get their own way? Manipulation is often thought to be a sophisticated skill that only develops after several years' experience and a lot of practice. In fact it is a very basic and primitive ability and even very young babies quickly learn to become expert in it. A good example of manipulation is when a baby cries, but then stops immediately it is picked up, only to start crying again as soon as it is put down, and then to stop when picked up once more. This is what manipulation is all about and the baby soon has the parents trained to give a cuddle or at least some sort of attention just by crying. After a bit more practice at manipulation, it doesn't take long before the child learns that being difficult in other ways, apart from crying, can also produce results!

It may sound as though a baby lies in the cot, thinking to itself, 'I wonder how I can get some attention by being difficult'. It isn't quite like that. The baby, just like any other person, has certain needs which, if not met, will result in some degree of distress and discomfort. It is the discomfort that leads on to the difficult behaviour and parents are very quick to respond because they know that something must be wrong and that their baby is so small and helpless. However, it is just this rapid response from parents that teaches children that crying or being difficult produces results and brings rewards. So you can see that children learn from a very young age that crying and difficult behaviour are good ways of making their needs known and getting their parents to do something for them. Crying and being difficult are therefore *very* normal in young children!

At what stage do children know right from wrong?

It doesn't seem right to say that a crying baby is being naughty and this is why parents make all those excuses and allowances when children are young. Of course, it is important to do this—for a while. But sooner or later, unless your child is very unusual, it will become quite clear that unreasonable demands are being made.

Naughtiness is something which starts to develop during the first year of life and then becomes more obvious when children have learnt the difference between 'yes' and 'no'. You can see this when a baby crawls towards something dangerous like an electric socket, stops and looks at you, and then carries on in spite of hearing you say 'no'. At this early stage there is no feeling of guilt for wrongdoing and it would be inappropriate to describe the child as naughty because a clear understanding of right and wrong is only just starting to develop. It is not until about 3 years of age that children show obvious feelings of guilt, but a clear understanding of right and wrong and the rules of every-day life doesn't really develop until 7–9 years of age.

This is much later than most parents would think, but the gradual evolution of a child's understanding of what bad behaviour is must be taken into account when you decide whether your child is being naughty or not. In addition to your child's stage of development and under-standing of right and wrong the following points should also be remembered when considering bad behaviour.

- Is the bad behaviour done on purpose or was it unintentional?
- Has the behaviour become an unconscious habit and therefore not deliberate?
- Does your child know for certain that the behaviour is unacceptable?
- Is the child just copying the bad behaviour of others in the family?
- Could the behaviour be a sign of illness or distress?
- Is the behaviour bad enough to discipline or is it best ignored?

There never seems to be enough time to work out the answers to these questions, but it is always helpful to sit

down and think about these points, especially if a particular pattern of behaviour is frequently repeated or if you
are not quite sure what to do about it.

So what is bad behaviour?

In the end it is parents who have to decide where to draw
the line between good and bad behaviour. This sounds
easy enough, but in reality there are several questions that
have to be sorted out first before a clear decision can be
reached:

- Is the behaviour likely to harm or upset other people?
- Do the parents agree?
- Is the decision right for the child's stage of develop-
  ment?
- Is the decision in line with what the rest of society
  expects?
- Have the same standards been adopted for the rest of
  the family?
- Has the child been given a simple explanation of the
  decision?
- Will close relatives and friends support the parent's
  decision?
- Can the decision be kept by all concerned?

How do you decide what is right and wrong? This is more
complicated than you might think because everyone has a
slightly different idea about it, which is why in a court of
law there is more than one person to make the decision.
Obviously it is necessary for parents to agree on what is
acceptable behaviour and on what limits will be set.

If parents can't agree with each other about where to
draw the line, then it would not be surprising if the
children were disobedient because they wouldn't know
what was expected of them. Children need to have a very
clear understanding of what exactly is required, other-

wise they will make their own rules and do whatever they want. Even if parents agree and have clear rules of behaviour for the family, it is still possible for friends and relatives to undermine this by open disagreement or a disapproving attitude. Equally, if parents set standards of behaviour which are very different from those at school and in the rest of society then again children will become confused about what is expected of them.

Testing the limits of what is and is not allowed is a normal stage of development and it will mean that children will frequently be overstepping the mark and behaving badly. It is therefore quite unreasonable to get angry with children during this period of learning which takes several years. It is also equally unreasonable to be too easy going and not to set clear standards of acceptable behaviour. If children are not given firm guidelines it will take an extra long time before they learn how far to go and when to stop.

Love and discipline

It may not be immediately obvious, but discipline and being strict can be a form of loving and caring. Children need to know what is right and wrong and need to have clear limits set on their behaviour. Discipline is about training and guiding children, and telling them exactly how far they can go. If you are able to be very consistent in limit-setting, your child will feel cared for and safe. However, this feeling of security will only occur if your limits are reasonable and fair for the stage of development that the child has reached. This is one of the many factors that make discipline so difficult: what is right at one age may be quite wrong at another. For example, allowing a 2-year-old to have a few tempers may not be unreasonable, but to let an older child indulge in tempers will only lead to more tantrums. Appropriate discipline and clear limit-setting is a way of protecting and loving your child.

Without this special type of care your child will have great difficulty in coping with the rough and tumble of everyday life and will become unpleasant to be with.

Fair, firm and consistent discipline is, therefore, a way of showing your love for your child and, like other forms of love, it frequently involves giving and self-sacrifice. In order to be consistent, parents have to work hard to agree with each other and to apply the agreed standards, even when they are tired and fed up or would rather be doing something else. In the same way that parental love and care makes children feel safe and happy, so good discipline helps children to feel secure and confident.

Your love will help your child feel happy, comfortable and good. Gradually this will help the child to develop self-confidence and a good self-image. In a very similar way, fair and consistent discipline will help your child to feel safe and secure, and eventually to develop self-discipline.

How can self-discipline be developed?

The ultimate aim of teaching children about right and wrong, good and bad, is so that they can learn how to control and manage their own behaviour and make their own decisions about where to set the limits. Discipline, like all other forms of teaching, is a slow and sometimes painful business. It has to be repeated often and 'refresher courses' may be necessary from time to time. It is no good being angry if your child seems to be slow in learning. Most of us will remember how difficult it is to learn from a teacher who is cross and shouts at you, and how helpful it is when the teacher is clear and repeats things until you understand.

The close links between discipline and teaching are seen in the way both schools and parents have in recent years tended to encourage children to learn for themselves from an early age. It is now known that this system only works if a child has already been taught a reasonable level of self-discipline and self-control, and for most children this isn't before the age of 7–8 years. Nursery schools that only offer free play and lack a firm structure and control of the children are not helping with self-discipline—they may be even be undermining what you are doing at home.

Children are not born with self-control and it will not develop unless you give firm and loving discipline in the early years. This is not at all easy because a necessary part of teaching is to allow your child the freedom to make mistakes. During the learning process children have to go from a state of high supervision and external control to very little, if their own inner control is to mature. It is a bit of a balancing act and here are some of the things that can go wrong:

- Children have very different personalities and some need firmer discipline than others.
- Some children are slow in their development and learning ability. They will require a high level of supervision and consistent limit-setting for much longer than usual.
- If your discipline is too tough and controlling, your child is likely to become too self-controlled and inhibited.
- Giving a high level of supervision and control for too long will lead to a child who is dependent and lacks self-confidence.
- Children who haven't had enough discipline when they were young usually lack self-control and cause unhappiness to themselves and others.

One way of looking at the task of teaching a child self-discipline is that it is a bit like learning to drive a car. You need a lot of supervision in the early stages and if your instructor doesn't have good control of the car you could easily have an accident. However, if the instructor does all the driving, you may never learn!

Conclusion

After all this it may seem as though being a parent and getting discipline just right for your child is virtually impossible. You're right, it is! So it is a good idea to be reasonably relaxed about any mistake you may make. Try and keep a sense of humour and realize that your child can learn from your mistakes as well!

CHAPTER 2

COPING WITH BAD BEHAVIOUR

Before you start

All children have their own unique way of being difficult and, because each is so varied, they will all require a type of discipline which is specially designed to meet their individual needs—what you might call 'designer discipline'! A lot of careful thought is necessary before you start to deal with bad behaviour. It is also necessary to take into account the circumstances in which the bad behaviour occurs. It isn't so much a case of a particular type of discipline being good or bad, it is more a question of what is best for your child in a given situation.

Before you start to discipline your child you should take into account the following four factors.

1. The child's personality

Sensitive children, who are easily upset, are usually very responsive to any kind of discipline and also to other people's moods. With this type of child it shouldn't be necessary to raise your voice much or even to be at all strict. If you are even a bit too cross, the sensitive child may become so upset that the point you were trying to correct gets lost and forgotten amongst the tears. On the other hand a tough, *thick-skinned* and rather insensitive child will require a very firm, clear and definite type of discipline. Any lack of clarity or indecision on the part of the parent

will be taken to mean that the child is free to behave well
or badly. The *moody and sulky* child will respond better to
discipline that is quickly over and done with, and where a
sense of humour is maintained so that things don't
become too serious. These are just a few examples to give
you some ideas, but you will have to work out for yourself
which type of discipline is best for your child.

2. The child's age
Younger children require very clear and straightforward
discipline with a high level of control. The words you use
should be simple and easily understood and physical
restraint may be necessary. *Older children* need a type of
discipline that encourages self-control and responsibility.
Explanations are required, with some discussion about
what the child should have done. Warnings and rewards
for good behaviour are helpful. *Teenagers* respond best to
discipline that is consistent and continues to maintain the
same family standards of behaviour. At the same time the
style of discipline should be non-authoritarian, where
there is some scope for negotiation and discussion.

3. Your personality
Your own personality is bound to affect how you manage
your children, but it is important that you don't let the
influence of your personality become too great. If you are a
quiet person by nature, you should be prepared to be a bit
more noisy and extrovert sometimes in order to make a
greater impact. If you tend to be a rather *emotional
person*, you may have more of an effect on your child if you
are quiet and controlled in your approach. Should you be a
short-tempered person, it will be important to try and
keep your cool and practise counting up to ten! On the
other hand, if you are an *easy going person* and don't mind
too much what your child does, it would probably help if
you became a bit stricter. A *loud, extrovert person* who is
always laughing and joking may have more effect by being
quiet and serious about discipline.

4. Your own childhood experience of discipline

One of the most surprising things about being a parent is the lasting effect that your own childhood has on you. It usually comes as quite a surprise to find yourself saying and doing exactly the same as your parents did to you. However, your upbringing may influence you in the opposite way so that you decide that there is no way you are going to put your child through what you experienced. Either way, you are still being influenced by your past.

The different types of discipline

What type of discipline do you use? It is a good idea to give this some thought. Are you soft and easy going, or are you a strict disciplinarian? Apart from the perfectly balanced and appropriate discipline that we all aim for, there are three main types of discipline:

1. Strict and authoritarian

The child isn't given the benefit of the doubt and very high standards of behaviour are set with little account being taken of the child's individual characteristics. Self-expression by the child is discouraged and the range of acceptable behaviour is restricted. As a result of a strict upbringing, children feel that they can't get away with bad behaviour. They become obedient and submissive, but may complain that they have been unfairly treated. Parents who are too strict run the risk of having inhibited children who may at some later stage become rebellious and resentful towards their parents and others in authority.

2. Easy going and indulgent

With soft and indulgent parents, children usually feel that they can do mostly what they like and have what they want. They come to believe that their own view is just as important as their parent's opinion. If someone says 'no you can't', they become distressed and angry. Children with parents who are too easy going seem to be self-confident and grown-up, treating adults like equals. Eventually the children become increasingly demanding and are told that they are too big for their boots or spoilt.

3. Inconsistent and unpredictable

This is the most common type of discipline and the most ineffective. However, we all do it because it is impossible to be consistent all the time. Because children are unable

to predict what will happen if they do something wrong, they become muddled and confused and in the end will usually do whatever they like.

Treating one child differently from another is a common form of inconsistency, but it can also be inconsistent to treat two children in the same way without taking into account their age and personality. What is right for one child may not be right for another with different needs.

If each parent sets different standards of behaviour for their child, even if the difference is a consistent one, the child will be unsure what is expected and will tend to take little notice of either parent. The parent who is the softer of the two will have great difficulty with discipline.

It isn't easy to keep discipline consistent each time you have to deal with naughty behaviour. Maybe you are feeling tired and fed up on one occasion and especially indulgent on another, but if your child can't rely on you to take the same line most of the time, don't expect all that much notice to be taken of what you say.

Most parents use a mixture of all three different types of discipline, but will tend to use one more than the others. Fortunately, so long as both parents are reasonably consistent, discipline has to be extremely strict or indulgent in order to cause any problems. It is inconsistency that is the most frequent cause of ineffective discipline, particularly where the parents set different standards of behaviour.

Agreement between parents is absolutely vital if discipline is going to be effective. If parents find that they differ in their approach, they will either have to agree to compromise and meet each other half way, or one parent will have to change and become more like the other in the type of discipline used and the standards that are set.

Although single parents don't have these problems in quite the same way, exactly the same issues arise if another adult joins the family, when there is a temptation to leave all disciplinary matters to the natural parent. It is a tremendous strain for a single parent to remain consistent all the time as well as working out what the best approach might be each time the child steps out of line.

Even if you have worked out and agreed on your family standards of behaviour at home, it is also important that there is a reasonable level of agreement between you and your child's school. If not, then once again you shouldn't be surprised if there are problems.

Grandparents and other relatives

Grandparents have much more influence on children than is generally appreciated. Make sure that they back up your discipline and don't undermine it by being overindulgent or critical. You may have to be very insistent with grandparents because they are likely to think that they know best! Here are some guidelines to consider when coping with grandparents who are interfering:

- Remember that you are the 'boss' now.
- It is 'safer' to be tough with your own parents than with your in-laws!
- You may have to lay down conditions for visiting.
- If there are problems, reduce the frequency and duration of each visit to whatever is tolerable.
- If all else fails, you may have to stop any visits for a while, but try and keep contact by letter or phone.
- A good relationship with grandparents is very helpful for children as they grow up and learn about their own family roots and about growing old; it is worth while making some sacrifices to achieve this.

Being fair

It is obviously important to try to be fair in the way that you discipline your child, but this is easier said than done. What you think is fair and reasonable may not seem that way to your child. Therefore, if anyone says that they think that you are not being fair, it is worth while finding out why, just to check whether they have a point. However, children often claim that they are being unfairly treated if they are feeling jealous or angry. Alternatively, they are just being manipulative.

It may sound surprising, but there is something to be said for *not* treating children absolutely equally and fairly all the time because life itself is often unfair and it is best to

IN THE LONG RUN YOU SHOULD TRY AND STRIKE A **REASONABLE BALANCE**....

learn this early on. In fact, if you try and treat children exactly the same, it usually makes them acutely aware of any small difference or inequality and increases feelings of jealousy and rivalry. However, in the long run you should try to strike a reasonable balance so that children don't come to feel that the world is against them.

Conclusion

There are many different types and styles of discipline, each of which can be effective if used in the right way, at the right time. Fortunately discipline doesn't have to be perfect all the time, so don't worry too much if you find it all rather difficult. There is quite a lot of scope for making mistakes without causing too many problems for your child. Most children, especially young ones, are remarkably resilient and tough, but maybe that is just as well!

CHAPTER 3

DIFFERENT METHODS OF DISCIPLINE

Rewards and praise

We all give a lot of praise and reward to babies and very small children and make excuses when they do something wrong. Certainly it is much more enjoyable to reward than to punish, but in spite of this, as children grow older we become considerably better at noticing bad behaviour and pay less attention to the good things that children do. Once your child has reached school age, try making a note of all the praise you have given in one day and measure it against all the times you have said 'don't' and been cross. You will probably be surprised how little praise and few rewards you give, when compared with tellings off and punishments. This is a shame because we all respond well to praise, even as adults!

Rewards come in many different forms and parents will have their own which seem to work with their child. Every reward has advantages and disadvantages and the main ones are outlined below:

Attention

Giving attention is the most important and the most effective of all rewards. Attention is much more effective if it is undivided and given without distraction or interruption, so that even a few seconds of undivided attention can be rewarding. However, it is surprisingly unusual for any child to have undivided attention. Parents are usually doing other things at the same time, such as washing up, cooking, watching TV, or just thinking about what needs to be done next.

Attention can be given in many different ways: a look, a smile, a touch, a cuddle or a few words may be all that is necessary. But if you want to make the attention really special, you will have to do something out of the ordinary and this is where special sessions of undivided attention can be very effective. It is a good idea to be rather formal about any special attention that you give for good behaviour because your child will take more notice of it. For example, rather than patting your child on the head and saying, 'well done', you could shake your child's hand or go into a separate room with strict instructions that you are not to be disturbed for a few minutes while you tell the child how pleased you are. Make a big thing of it and you will be amazed at how it is enjoyed.

Remember that attention doesn't have to be given for very long, provided it is undivided and enjoyable. A few minutes will do.

Unfortunately, children are usually given much more attention for being naughty than for being good, with the inevitable risk that a child's behaviour will become steadily worse in order to get even more attention. It is important to check frequently that you are taking more notice of your child for being good than for being bad (a bit like checking the oil level in the engine of your car!) If the level of attention that you are giving for good behaviour is low, your child might start making a lot of noise or doing something bad in order to be noticed. In which case you will have to specially look out for good things that your child has done so that you can give the extra praise and attention.

Always remember that the attention you give to your child is more effective and in the end more wanted by children than any other kind of reward. All it costs is a little time.

Praise

Parents are brilliant at giving children praise and appreciation for the first few years, but as children grow older less and less praise is given until in adult life it is quite a rare event. When did somebody last tell you what a marvellous parent you are? We all look for clues that tell us we are doing all right. This is one of the reasons why we care so much about what other people think of our children.

As children grow older you will need to become more discriminating in your praise, because it is important that children learn to assess what they have done in a realistic way. You can help your child to do this by giving selective praise and occasional constructive criticism. Imagine a pair of scales with praise for your child in one pan and criticism in the other. Praise should always outweigh criticism, otherwise there is a high risk of your child developing a bad self-image.

Special treats and privileges

Treats are frequently given as a reward for good behaviour, but they are no substitute for attention or praise. It is, however, much easier to hand out a sweet or a toy than to devote time and energy to giving attention. It is best to use treats as a way of backing up and strengthening any praise you give, so that if you give a treat to your child for being good, always give praise at the same time.

It is best to avoid giving food as a reward. Although your child may be pleased at the time, the end result is likely to be a poor appetite at the next meal and, in the long run, an increase in weight. An obese child has a vast range of problems which include teasing, increased frequency of illness and accidents, and a shorter life expectancy. So giving food as a reward may actually turn into a punishment in the end. However, it is very easy for your child to develop the habit of expecting food as a reward and then for this habit to continue into adult life. If you are going to use food to reward good behaviour then try using fruit or even raw vegetables!

Drinks can also be used as a reward, but they have the same problems as food. Perhaps it is best to have one or two things that you use regularly as a reward and keep them just for special treats in order to make them more desirable and rewarding.

...AND AS A SPECIAL TREAT FOR BEING SO GOOD, YOU CAN HAVE A SLICE OF RAW CARROT AND DO THE WASHING UP.... HOW ABOUT THAT!!

PRIVILEGES ARE **EVERYDAY** ACTIVITIES THAT YOU MAKE **SPECIAL**...

Bribery

Bribery sounds rather nasty and unfortunately parents sometimes avoid offering rewards for good behaviour because they think it is bribery. If you are worried about bribery simply change the word 'bribe' into 'reward' and you should feel much better! Don't say: 'I will bribe you with a treat to be good'; say instead 'I will *reward* you with a treat if you are good'.

Love and affection

It is important for children to know that they are loved even though they can do bad things. In other words, it should be possible to love your child while at the same time hating what they do wrong. There is much less risk of damaging a child's self-esteem if a distinction is made between the person and the bad deed.

Obviously, love and affection have a powerful influence on all of us and it is possible to use them as rewards. However, using love as a reward has its risks because children might come to believe that they are only loved when they are good and since most of us spend a lot of time *not* being good, children may easily feel that they are unloved. Therefore it is important to keep the love and affection going all the time, even if you don't always feel like it. An unloved child will feel bad and eventually will probably be bad.

Fortunately, it isn't necessary for parents to have wonderful loving feelings for their children all the time in order to do a good job. In fact, many parents feel quite hateful towards them at times and a few parents have little affection for their children. In spite of this it is possible to show care and affection without necessarily feeling it.

So long as you are aware of the possible danger of using affection as a reward, there is no harm in giving children a little extra love and care when they do something good. An extra hug, kiss, stroke or touch, together with a few words of praise, can be very effective and the physical contact reinforces what you say.

Punishments

In theory it should be possible to avoid all punishments by only rewarding good behaviour and taking no notice of bad behaviour. In practice it isn't possible—you would have to be a saint to do it!

The main problem with punishment is to find something that fits the crime both in severity and in appropriateness. Another difficulty is that it is easy to overdo punishments because you are so keen for your child to be good and because it is easy to get carried away in the heat of the moment, especially if you are feeling very angry. The result of too much punishment is an angry and resentful child, who feels bad, but behaves well until adolescence when they tend to become difficult, disobedient and delinquent. However, children who have had too little discipline may also become difficult, disobedient and delinquent in adolescence. So it is important to get discipline as balanced as possible from the very beginning.

Punishments come in many different forms. Here are some of them.

Smacking

It is very easy to smack a child who has done something naughty. It doesn't require much effort, you don't have to think about it and it is immediately effective in the short run. However, as children grow older, smacking quickly becomes less effective and by the time your child goes to school it will usually make things worse rather than better and tend to build up a feeling of resentment in your child.

A quick tap on the back of the hand may be helpful in the first year or two of a child's life as a means of reinforcing what you say, especially about anything dangerous. For example, if your child continues to try and put a finger in the electric socket, a sharp 'no' accompanied by a smack on the hand when next this happens should help to get the message across. At that age there is no point in telling them about the inherent danger in acting as an earth conductor for high-voltage current! Equally, giving praise for not touching the socket would probably make the child more likely to think that the socket might be really interesting and therefore want to investigate the socket even more closely.

The main problem with physical punishment is that it encourages children to sort out their own problems and frustrations in a physical way themselves, by hitting and punching other people when they are angry with them. A good rule of thumb is that you should stop using smacking as a punishment as soon as your child is old enough to hit you back—that is, around 2 years of age. You may think that is very young to stop smacking, or you may even think that is it wrong to smack a child whatever the age. It is important for each family to work out from the very beginning what the rules are going to be for smacking. Both parents must agree on the rules, otherwise their discipline will be undermined and the smack will have no effect or may even be harmful.

Most parents find that they occasionally feel driven to smack a much older child when they have done something really bad. Do try to avoid it if you possibly can, particularly if you are feeling angry, because it can so easily get out of control, leaving both you and your child upset and angry.

Whatever you do, NEVER, NEVER smack your child with anything other than your open hand and then only on your child's hand or possibly lower leg. If you use any object or a fist to smack your child with, you won't be able to gauge how hard you have hit your child. There is a considerable risk of causing physical damage to your child, which is a form of child abuse, but there is also a risk that excessive smacking will cause emotional damage, which is another form of child abuse. We all get uncomfortably angry with our children from time to time, so it is important to think about these things even if they are distasteful.

Remember that smacking is increasingly dangerous and ineffective as your child gets older and that to give more than one firm smack on any occasion is an indulgence on your part. Well, nobody said it was easy being a parent!

Shouting

Shouting, like smacking, is easy to do but it soon loses

effect and you will find yourself shouting louder and louder until in the end you are screaming, and that isn't much fun for anyone—particularly the neighbours!

If you are going to shout, it is more effective to do it early on, rather than to have a gradual build-up. This slow build-up teaches children to take no notice of you, because they know from experience that there is no need to do what you say until you get really worked up. If you were to make a tape recording of your shouting, you would probably get a terrible shock because it sounds so awful. It is therefore best to reserve your shouting for desperate situations. At least your child will take some notice of you then.

Rather than using up your energy shouting, it is sometimes surprisingly effective to *whisper* very quietly so that your child has to strain to hear. In this way the child is actually more likely to hear what you say. Obviously it is unlikely to work if you whisper all the time; it is the change from the usual shouting that has the effect. If you do whisper, it will be more effective if you speak with a lot of emphasis and in a clipped tone of voice.

Nagging

If your child isn't immediately obedient it is normal to repeat the same instruction again. . . and again. . . and again; in other words, to nag. The trouble with nagging is that it is ineffective, but in spite of this most parents keep on nagging and hoping for a miracle!

What nagging does is to train children to take no notice of what you say because they know that you are going to say it again and again. Nagging also means that you will gradually work yourself up into a state and eventually most parents lose their temper and start shouting. This usually takes children by surprise, because what started the nagging was something that was not very important at all. Another problem about nagging is that it gets children into the habit of waiting until you start shouting and getting cross, so that they soon learn that there is no need to do anything before the shouting starts.

The golden rule about nagging is: DON'T! If you catch yourself doing it, either stop and say no more, or go straight into the shouting/cross phase.

It is a good idea to set yourself the target of only saying things once. If your child doesn't do what you ask immediately, then give a warning. If this still produces no result, then absolutely insist that the child does whatever it is that you have asked. This may mean that you have to get extremely angry and actually make your child do it. The advantage of this approach is that you miss out all the nagging that normally occurs before you become cross and you are putting on a show of being angry before you are pushed to the point of losing your temper and being out of control. At the same time your child is learning that you mean what you say and that it is no good just switching off and taking no notice of what you are saying.

Removing attention

Withdrawing attention is one of the most effective ways of punishing a child and yet this method is rarely used to the full by parents. If your child is doing something very naughty it will of course be difficult if not impossible to ignore it. But most of the time it should be possible, especially if you are sure that your child is safe and can't do much damage if a temper develops.

A strong nerve and a good sense of timing are needed if you are going to ignore a naughty child. If you remove attention from your child for too short a time, it will have no effect, but there is a real danger of ignoring a child for too long. If you do this your child will forget what has been done wrong and begin to feel angry with you instead. Just a few minutes should be long enough and the younger the child is, the shorter the time should be.

Sending a child to another room is a common punishment which removes attention from the child. There are three parts to this punishment:

1. The loss of your attention. This effect wears off in a few minutes.
2. A recovery time for you: 5–10 minutes should be enough.
3. An apology from your child and a discussion of what went wrong.

Many parents make the mistake of thinking that the longer a child stays in the room, the greater the punishment is. This is not the case, because shortly after arriving in the bedroom the naughty child will find something to play with and start to have fun. If you send a child to the bedroom for too long, you end up with a child who blames you for being unreasonable, rather than a child who feels guilty and apologetic.

The recovery time allows you to cool down and feel able to have another go at coping with a naughty child. It is important to remember that any time over 2–3 minutes is for your benefit and is no longer a punishment for your child, while anything over about 10 minutes will breed resentment and make things worse for you in the long run.

As soon as the punishment is finished, the naughty child should apologize for whatever was wrong. Don't expect the apology to be done perfectly, with the right tone of voice and a guilty expression. Just saying, 'I am sorry' should be enough, even if it said with a grumpy voice. Apart from reminding children that they have done something wrong, the apology teaches an important social skill and helps to bring the episode to a close. In this way the bad feelings are left behind and a new start can be made.

Sometimes children are so naughty that they refuse to leave the room when you send them to their bedroom. If your children are small and you are large it is reasonable to physically remove them to the bedroom, but with older children this isn't possible, in which case you could either turn your back on them and be silent or you could leave the room yourself.

Loss of privileges

Going to bed early, being kept in, and stopping TV are examples of lost privileges which can be used effectively as punishments, but here again it is important to get the timing and extent of the lost privilege just right. Too little has no effect, too much causes anger. Parents should be careful not to stop their children from doing things that they would actually like them to do. For instance, if you want your child to learn to swim, don't stop swimming as a punishment. If you want your child to be sociable, don't ban friends from the house.

Here are some examples of how you can stop privileges in an effective way:

- Stopping 5 minutes of a favourite TV programme or doing something nice for a shorter time than usual is often more effective than not having it at all.
- Remember to select an appropriate privilege—some children actually like staying in or going to bed early.
- Try to make the loss of privilege occur as soon after the bad behaviour as possible—if it is delayed too long your child will forget what it was all about.
- It is possible to invent a privilege to stop, for example: 'Oh dear! I was going to ask if you would like me to play a game with you, but we won't be able to do this now!'.
- Prolonged loss of privilege will cause resentment, so try to keep it in proportion to the 'crime'. For example, if your daughter comes home 30 minutes after you said that she should, then keep her in for exactly the same time the next day—if she comes back late again the next day too, then you just add that time onto the 30 minutes.

Being angry and telling off

Being cross and angry with a child can be a very severe punishment and quite sufficient in itself. However, it has to be impressive to be effective, which means that you will have to put on a convincing act, but not go over the top. If you become too angry, your child may think, 'Well this is ridiculous—they must be flipping their lid poor things!' In other words your child comes to blame you for being too angry and forgets what has been done wrong.

OH... ARE YOU A BIT CROSS MUMMY?...

YOU MAY HAVE TO PUT ON AN **AWARD WINNING PERFORMANCE** TO HAVE ANY EFFECT....

If your child is rather sensitive and highly strung there will be no need to get very angry and there may even be a danger of upsetting the child too much. As a result you will have an obedient but anxious and inhibited child. On the other hand, if your child is thick-skinned you may have to put on an award-winning performance to have any effect. Judging the right level of anger for each child on each occasion is a skill that most parents take years to develop, so don't give up or upset yourself if you can't always get it right.

Making discipline work

There are many different ways of dealing with bad behaviour and it is easy to try one method and give up too quickly if it doesn't work immediately.

It may well be that the method itself is all right but it isn't being applied in a *consistent* way. Discipline is all about *communication*, i.e. giving a clear message to children so that everyone knows that you are serious and that you mean what you say. Although most discipline is based on either giving rewards for good behaviour or punishing bad behaviour, none of this will work unless it is done with loving concern and *care*. Equally, you can't expect to have much effect unless your child *clearly* understands what you are getting at. Clear, consistent communication is helped if it is done with *conviction*. But even if you manage to do all this, you may still not have much success unless you *constantly* stick at it. We therefore have the six Cs of effective discipline:

Constantly Communicate Clearly with Consistency, Conviction and Care!

It sounds easy and straightforward doesn't it? However, most of us need a lot of practice before we get it right, and, as with most other skills, a lot of hard work is necessary to be able to communicate clearly to your child that you are serious and that you mean what you say.

How to be a good communicator

Communication has many different components that need to be used together if your message is going to get through to your child. Consider the following check-list:

- to start with you must have your child's full attention
- make sure that your child is looking at your face

- the look in your eyes must show that you mean what you say
- your tone of voice must be firm and incisive
- the words you use must be short and to the point
- each word should be very clearly spoken with conviction
- use gestures like pointing or wagging your finger to back up what you are saying
- your manner must be confident and determined.

Don't expect to get it right the first time: most parents require a lot of practice. You will quickly find out whether your act is any good or not by the response. If little notice is taken then more practice is needed, although it could conceivably be that your performance is wonderful and there is something wrong with your child. If you are not sure which way round it is, ask friends to watch your act and see if it impresses them!

Conclusion

Praise and encouragement are more effective in the long run than punishments, and children require different styles of discipline specially designed to meet their own unique needs. If the balance of 'do's and 'don't's and of rewards and punishments isn't right and is tipped towards criticism and being negative and hostile, then your child will let you know either by becoming progressively more difficult or by being anxious and withdrawn. Only a few parents find it easy to get discipline right and most of us have to keep working hard at it for years and years, so don't give up—KEEP AT IT!

CHAPTER 4

SPECIAL TECHNIQUES

Here are some techniques that you can use to back up your discipline and make it more effective. The methods are well known, but have to be used correctly to produce any results, so I will explain each one in some detail.

Prevention is better than cure

There are a lot of things you can do to avoid your child being difficult and disobedient. Obviously, being firm and clear in your discipline will make naughty behaviour less likely to occur, but here are some other points to consider.

Setting a good example

Children quickly learn to follow the example set by older children and adults whom they respect. In fact, setting a good example is one of the best ways of achieving good behaviour and avoiding the need to use discipline. It is always important to be careful that you're not punishing your child for something that you do or that someone else in the family does and gets away with. This would be unfair and undermine your discipline.

Supervision

A great deal of bad behaviour occurs when children are

unsupervised and away from your watchful eye. This is one way of finding out how successful you have been in setting standards of behaviour. If you hear that your child is well behaved when away from you at school or with friends, then you know that you are doing a pretty good job!

Young children need almost total supervision during the daytime, but as they grow older it can be difficult to know how quickly to ease off and allow more freedom. In fact, the only way of finding this out is by trial and error. It is important to gradually build up trust and give your child increasingly more responsibility.

With the distractions of the radio and TV and the demands of everyday life, it is easy to cut down on supervision and to give children too much freedom too early. So if you or other people find your child's behaviour difficult or disruptive, an increase in adult supervision is the first thing you should consider. It may well be that your child's naughtiness has more to do with lack of adequate supervision than with a need for more discipline. Have a think about it!

Organizing the environment

A lot of bad behaviour can be prevented by arranging your home so that it is safe for children. Here are some ideas for 'structuring the environment' to make it less likely that your child will do something naughty:

- use a playpen for children up to 2 years old
- put your favourite ornaments out of harm's way
- keep the TV, video and hi-fi out of reach, unless you don't mind the knobs being fiddled with
- use a box or cupboard to keep toys safe

and for older children:

- put an alarm on the larder door if food goes missing!
- don't leave money lying around
- avoid your child having too many toys to get lost or broken
- insist on headphones if the music is too loud

These are just a few ideas to show you how you might go about organizing your home to make life easier for you and so that you don't have to be cross with your child quite so frequently.

Habit training

Getting dressed and undressed, washing, sitting at the table for meals, going to the toilet, and going to bed occur every day and frequently cause arguments. These disputes can be avoided by training your child from an early age to accept the events as a regular routine so that they become an automatic part of everyday life that requires no discussion or thought—in other words they become a habit.

If your child is causing problems with two or more of these daily tasks, it is probably best to look at it as a habit-training problem. In which case you will have to be much more insistent and firm about keeping to a regular routine and doing things in the same way each day in order to get a good habit established. If this doesn't work you need to be even more insistent and do everything by the clock. It is well worth keeping at it until you have got it right, because in this way you will avoid all the difficult behaviour which occurs several times each day.

'At risk' times

Children are much more likely to be naughty and disruptive if they are bored, hungry, thirsty, or tired. All of these conditions can be avoided with some advance planning and thought. Again, it is helpful to have a regular daily routine that avoids these problems, by planning meals, snacks, playtimes, and rests. A special 'at risk' time is when children return from school, so it is a good idea to have a snack and a quiet relaxing time for a short while as soon as children arrive home from school.

Other 'at risk' times are just before meals and last thing at night. These are times when it is important to keep children occupied, perhaps by getting them to help you or by organizing some other activity for them. Remember that you also have 'at risk' times when you are tired, hungry, physically ill or feeling fed up and miserable.

The art of timing

In order to be really effective, rewards and punishments

have to be timed to occur immediately after the relevant behaviour, sometimes called *the target behaviour*. In this way your child is able to make the link between the behaviour and what you think of it. The longer the gap between the target behaviour and your response, the less likely it is that what you do or say will have any effect.

If you return home and hear that your child has done something bad, your natural reaction is to be upset and angry. Try to change your feeling of being upset into sadness rather than anger, because in this situation sadness is much more effective and it will allow you to have a quiet talk with your child about what went wrong and how the naughty behaviour can be avoided in future. Delayed praise from the returning parent can also be effective in backing up what has been said about good behaviour that occurred earlier in the day.

There are occasions when the time isn't right to discipline your child. For example, on a special occasion, that would be spoilt by having to be cross or where your child might feel humiliated to be disciplined in front of friends. In these cases it is best to leave it until a more appropriate time and then discuss the event with your child and express sadness rather than anger. Another time when it may be best not to discipline children is when they are ill, but here again timing is all important because it is vital to judge the correct time for restarting discipline. If you leave it too late your child could become a little monster in no time at all. If you get it right, the return to normal discipline is a very reassuring sign to your child that he or she is getting better.

To punish a child is always a sad event which is distressing for all concerned. It is therefore a good idea to spend some time and effort making things right afterwards. When you feel that the time is right, discuss briefly with your child what has happened, so that they can learn from the episode (3 or 4 minutes is quite long enough). Children should learn to apologize for their bad behaviour as this helps to make them more aware that they are responsible for it and that they can't put the blame on someone else. However, it is good to set an example to your child by apologizing if you have gone a bit over the top or done something wrong.

Perhaps the most important aspect of timing discipline is knowing when to stop. Most parents give up rather easily when the method of discipline that they are using doesn't seem to be working. Don't give up, but rather think, am I doing it right? If you think that you are, then keep at it! The methods of discipline that I have described in this book can be expected to bring about an obvious improvement in 4–6 weeks if you apply them correctly, consistently, and confidently. Perfection takes a little longer!

Star charts and records

Keeping a diary or record of naughty behaviour can be very helpful if you're not quite sure why your child is being disobedient and difficult. Often the reason will become clear when you, or perhaps someone else reads your observations. It may be helpful to use the ABC method of recording as follows:

A = antecedents, i.e. whatever happened before the behaviour
B = behaviour, i.e. the naughty behaviour
C = consequence, i.e. what happened as a result of the behaviour.

The ABC method is a good way of helping you to think about what exactly caused an episode of bad behaviour and it is not unusual for parents to find that they are actually keeping the problem behaviour going without realizing it, for example by giving in to children who behave badly. After a week or two you may see a pattern emerging which will show you what is going wrong and may give you ideas as to how to change things to improve the behaviour.

Star charts give a less detailed record of behaviour and don't have to involve stars at all. The chart divides the day up into separate periods. If the child is good during any period, a star is put on the chart to show that the behaviour was good. If the child has been bad then the chart space is left blank. However, instead of stars you can use ticks, smiley faces, little drawings, stickers or anything else that appeals to the child.

The idea behind a chart is very simple—rewarding good behaviour—and it may seem artificial. However, there is more to a chart than you might think:

- The stars may become very powerful rewards in themselves.
- The focus is changed from the bad behaviour to concentrating on good behaviour.
- A chart diverts attention and anger away from people and onto the chart.
- A chart helps parents to be more consistent.
- The chart acts as a record of what progress is being made.

Children between the ages of 5 and 12 usually respond well to charts, but it is important to make it into something special and interesting and to involve your child in the organization of the chart as much as possible. Try to make it good fun and something that your child can be proud of.

The chart should be divided into periods that are short enough for your child to remain well behaved—with a bit of effort on a good day—so that it is not too difficult to gain a star. At the end of the day, provided your child has tried to be good, there should be more stars than spaces. As soon as you feel that your child has got the message and is regularly being well behaved, the stars should be made a bit more difficult to achieve. This can be done by gradually increasing the duration of each period or by expecting more from the child before a star is gained. Whichever way round it is, your child must at all times know exactly what has to be done to achieve a star.

One of the most difficult things with a chart is to keep it going and keep your child motivated. You will need all your ingenuity to keep your child interested in the chart. Here are some ideas:

- Put the chart in a prominent position such as the kitchen or dining room wall.
- Involve other family members or friends in praising the child for any success.
- Give the stars a value, e.g. 1p per star, or 5 stars gain the child a privilege such as staying up a bit later one night, having a story read, or playing a game. Don't make the stars worth too much, otherwise it can get completely out of hand!

Most charts work well for a day or two but then things slip back into the bad old ways unless you work hard to keep the chart going. Aim to have the chart for a fairly short time, such as 1–4 weeks. If things are no better by the end of this period, try reading the Help! section on page 86.

Pocket money

As soon as your child has some understanding of the value of money, it is helpful to give a small amount of pocket money. Pocket money is useful for the following reasons:

- teaching the value of money
- learning to delay gratification
- teaching children that actions have consequences
- giving a child the feeling of being more independent
- to increase self-control
- to encourage saving
- to teach your child about giving and generosity.

Clearly there are other ways of achieving the same goals, but pocket money is convenient and can be very effective if managed correctly. It is best to keep the money limited to a small amount and then gradually increase it as your child grows older. At the same time children should be expected to do more with the money and to be more responsible for their own needs and for buying gifts for others.

One way of organizing the amount of pocket money would be to start with 10p at 5 years old and increase by 10p a year up to 10 years of age. Then increase by 20p a year up to 15 years of age and finally at 15 years old start a clothing allowance which can cover other things as well. There is no point in giving large amounts of pocket money, because the more you give the more your child will want. There will always be someone else that your child knows who gets more money and they will be quoted to you whenever your child wants more money, but don't be fooled by this ploy. However, it is important that you help your child to feel content with the pocket money and to use it wisely, rather than spending all the time feeling envious of others and grumbling for more money.

When your child is older, a clothing allowance can be very helpful in encouraging independence and responsibility. It is a good idea to set the amount low to begin with and then review it after 3–6 months. Meanwhile your teenager should keep a detailed record of every item bought and then present it to you with the receipts at the end of the review period. If you are satisfied that all is well, then you can consider whether an increase is justified or not. It may be best for you to buy the clothes for school so that at least you know that the basics are all right.

Once you have got the pocket money well established, it can then be used for discipline in the following ways:

- If your child does something good then there could be a small bonus with the pocket money at the end of the week.
- Doing something bad can be dealt with by a deduction from pocket money, but young children may not remember what they did wrong if the time gap is too

large between the event and the deduction.

- If you have made a deduction of pocket money for whatever reason, it is a good idea to hand your child the full amount each week and then get them to hand back the required amount. This will help your child to be fully aware of what the deduction was all about.

- Be careful not to undermine the pocket money by giving extra things that should normally be bought by your child. It can be very revealing to add up the cost of all the extra treats you give during one week—you will probably get quite a surprise!

- Many children are impulsive and even reckless with their pocket money when it first starts and it all goes in a few days. If this is the case, it may help for your child to be given the money more frequently, perhaps twice a week, but preferably not every day because this won't encourage your child to learn how to control money and delay gratification.

- Pocket money can be used for paying fines for bad behaviour, but it is especially useful for paying towards the cost of breakages and damage caused deliberately by your child or through carelessness. This helps children to become more aware of the consequences of their actions and helps you to deal with the situation without becoming too upset and angry.

- It may also be helpful to have a savings account to accompany the pocket money. Not only does this encourage saving, it is also useful as back-up for buying special items or paying off fines quickly.

- Any extra money given by friends and relatives is best collected and put into your child's savings account, otherwise the money will probably be frittered away.

- One parent should take responsibility for organizing the pocket money to make sure that it is given regularly and that deductions are made when necessary.

- Try to avoid stopping the money completely. Even prisoners have a small amount of pocket money!

'Time Out'

The procedure for removing attention and isolating children when they have been naughty is sometimes called 'Time Out', which is a technical term for excluding a child from having any attention or reward. It is a form of punishment that is particularly popular in America, but even so I don't think there is any evidence that American children are any better behaved than other children. So Time Out doesn't perform miracles, but it can be useful. In fact parents often use a form of Time Out without realizing it when they send a child out of the room or to bed early for doing something naughty.

Time Out should be carried out on a carefully planned basis, where you start by identifying a specific, unacceptable behaviour, *the target behaviour*, and then planning how you will remove attention in a predetermined way whenever the bad behaviour is observed. There are two main varieties of Time Out that parents can use.

1. Attention Time Out in a separate room. Here children are removed from the situation in which they are behaving badly and sent or taken to a room where they will get no attention. They are then left there for a specific number of minutes. Alternatively, you can remain in the room but ignore your child or you can leave the room yourself.
2. Activity Time Out. Here children are not allowed to join in a particular activity, or told to stop whatever they were doing. They aren't asked to leave the room, but are expected to remain to see what is being missed.

The period of isolation should be timed by the clock and is usually for a few minutes only. One minute per year of age would be a reasonable guide. However, the main impact of Time Out is in the first few seconds when children realize that the parent is displeased to the point of wanting to ignore them. The Time Out procedure is then repeated as often as it is necessary to have the desired effect. Here are some ways of making sure that Time Out is effective when you use it:

- Decide in advance which room is going to be the place where you send or take your child to for Time Out. The room must be completely safe for your child to be left unsupervised for a few minutes. Usually the bedroom is a suitable place.
- Make sure that you time the period of Time Out accurately and stick to what you have decided.
- Sending your child out of the room may be just as effective as isolating him or her in another room.
- Even turning your back on your child can be an effective form of Time Out.
- Your child must be quite clear which bad behaviour it is that you are 'timing out' and it is best to work on one specific bad behaviour at a time, or your child might

spend most of the day in Time Out!

- When the Time Out is completed, an apology from your child is a good way of signalling that the episode is over and done with.
- It is best to put aside any discussion about the event until quite a while after the Time Out.
- You can make the most of Time Out by not becoming cross or emotional. In fact, Time Out works best if you are firm and tough, and when you are able to keep your temper.

There are many problems in using this rather rigid approach to discipline. Even the name 'Time Out' tends to give the impression of a technical procedure and it is sometimes used to describe an extreme type of more prolonged and total isolation which is not appropriate for a family home. Here are some of the problems to watch out for when using Time Out:

- Some children actually prefer to spend some time away from the situation which they have caused. In this case the Time Out is a reward and will have the reverse effect of that intended.
- Other children may resist being 'timed out' and continue to behave badly and to attract even more attention. In this case another type of discipline would be better, especially one that uses rewards.
- Time Out only teaches children what they should NOT do, rather than what they SHOULD do. So don't forget to tell your child exactly what sort of behaviour you would like and, if you get it, don't forget to praise it!
- If the Time Out is too long your child is likely to become angry and resentful and forget what the Time Out is for.
- The Time Out must occur immediately after the bad behaviour if it is to be effective. Delayed or repeated Time Out for one episode of bad behaviour sows seeds of resentment.

- Time Out is difficult to organize when you are away from home. If you do carry it out, don't forget to warn everyone first, otherwise they may wonder what you are up to!
- If you use Time Out too frequently it will lose its effect, so use it sparingly and concentrate on one particular naughty behaviour at a time.

Special diets

The idea that you are what you eat is both attractive and fashionable. Many parents have had the experience of excluding food additives, red meat, milk, wheat germ and other food stuffs from their children's diet and noticing an improvement in behaviour. It is therefore surprising that almost all the well conducted scientific research has shown that food additives and normal foods make no difference to behaviour. Could it be that all this research, carried out in many different countries round the world, has somehow got it wrong?

A likely explanation for the positive effect of dietary restrictions is that parents are usually very strict about it and perhaps for the first time say 'no' to their child in a firm and definite way. Certainly it is not unusual for disciplinary control in one area to improve a child's general behaviour.

If you still want to try to see whether a change of diet will help, it is important to do it properly. This means conducting your own experiment, which needs to be done in 2-week stages. This is because changes of behaviour are said to take about two weeks to respond to alterations in diet. Here are some guidelines:

- Keep a daily record of your child's behaviour.
- Remove the suspect foods completely for two weeks.
- If an exclusion diet appears to help, then go on to the next stage.
- Replace one food at a time at 2-week intervals and if

the behaviour becomes worse again it can be excluded from the diet for a longer period.

- When you have decided on the final diet, make sure that it isn't unbalanced. Get professional advice if you are in any doubt. Some special diets can cause nutritional deficiencies.
- It is a good idea to use an independent observer who doesn't know what diet your child is on, but observes the changes in behaviour, just to be quite sure that you aren't imagining any improvement.
- You may be able to gradually get your child back to a reasonably normal diet, so it is worthwhile reintroducing the excluded foods from time to time, just to check if they are tolerated without a deterioration of behaviour.

Keeping a sense of humour

The whole business of discipline can get a bit heavy and serious if you are not careful. Try to keep a sense of humour about discipline—it's much more fun! A humorous punishment can sometimes be more effective than a serious one because your child is more likely to remember and learn from it. A sense of humour is a very personal thing, so you will have to think up your own kind of funny discipline. The joke is as much for you to enjoy as for your child, because it will help you to stay relatively calm and not lose your temper. Discipline carried out in a temper is very rarely effective for more than a few minutes, so have a bit of fun instead!

Conclusion

Discipline is a form of training and is essential if you want your child to become socially acceptable and to develop self-control. The emphasis should be on learning to do the right thing, rather than just stopping bad behaviour. Start from the very beginning with firm, strong discipline so that your child learns what the limits are: this is an important way of showing your loving care. As your child grows up and by behaving well earns more responsibility, you can then allow more freedom. Although there are many useful methods of discipline, the most important thing is to be confident in what you do and to follow things through, but above all try not to lose that sense of humour!

TRY TO KEEP A **SENSE OF HUMOUR** ABOUT DISCIPLINE....

CHAPTER 5

BAD BEHAVIOUR: QUESTIONS AND ANSWERS

Yes but . . .

'My son has been difficult from the moment he was born and I don't seem to be able to change his bad behaviour. What should I do?'

It is increasingly recognized that some babies are born with a difficult temperament. The so-called *'difficult child'* is easy to identify, because he or she has the following characteristics right from the start:

- *unpredictable;* usually difficult to feed, put to bed or to toilet and then sometimes easy
- *very strong emotions;* with tempers and crying, rather than being happy
- *easily disturbed by change;* slow to settle and difficult to comfort.

It sounds as though you have a child with a difficult temperament, in which case you will immediately recognize these characteristics. If this is the case, you have a tough time ahead of you! But don't despair, there are things that you can do to help your child and many children will have grown out of it before they start at school. Many children will fit the description given above, but it is possible to distinguish between children who are born with a difficult temperament and other children who have been allowed to learn how to get attention and get their own way by being difficult, because the problems are present from birth in the former case and not in the latter.

These children with a difficult temperament require 'extra super' parenting if they are to be helped, so it is not going to be easy. They need more of the following than you would normally provide:

- routine and regularity
- clear limit setting
- high level of supervision
- firm, consistent, loving discipline
- frequent comfort and reward.

If you are able to provide this extra care, most children will learn to modify their temperament reasonably well by the time they start at school. But some children will continue to be difficult with behaviour problems and then it is just a case of carrying on with the guidelines above with determination and increased intensity.

It is most important to balance this rather controlling form of care with a great deal of positive care and love. Otherwise you will find that you are forever getting at your child and saying things like: 'stop it', 'be quiet', 'come here' or 'don't'. Many parents find it difficult to be loving towards a child who is frequently irritable and disobedient. Your son will probably have many bad experiences because he is naughty, so you will have to work at it. Here are some ways of balancing the negative experiences that a child with a difficult temperament will go through.

- Try to avoid situations which you know your son will be unable to cope with without being very difficult and temperamental. These occasions only give children practice in how to be difficult and annoying! However, if it is something like getting dressed in the morning or going to the toilet, you obviously can't avoid it. In this case, a regular routine is helpful so that your child becomes used to doing things automatically, and knows that arguments and tempers are pointless.

- Look out for any good thing that your son does, especially if he manages to control his temper in a satisfactory way; also give as much praise as you can. Don't worry about going over the top with your praise, it won't do any harm!

DON'T WORRY ABOUT GOING **OVER THE TOP** WITH YOUR PRAISE....

- Deliberately set up situations with which you know your son should be able to cope without being difficult and behaving badly so that you can give praise and encouragement, rather than telling him off yet again.
- Arrange special times for your son to be alone with you or with another trusted adult, purely to enjoy your time together. This is *High Quality Time* which is many times more worthwhile than being together in the ordinary way, when you have something else to do at the time, for example the washing up, the cleaning or making a meal.

'What can I do with my daughter who always seems to be doing naughty things?'

I assume that you have decided that your daughter doesn't have a difficult temperament like the boy in the previous question. Even so, the same guidelines will help, together with all the things I have outlined in the book. If your daughter is aged 7 years or older, it may be that she has developed a bad self-image, which in turn will lead to bad behaviour. The main signs of a poor self-image are as follows:

- deliberately doing bad things in an obvious way in order to get caught
- seeming to get pleasure from being told off
- appearing to be uncomfortable when praised
- deliberately spoiling anything that is good
- talking about being bad and not feeling as good as other children.

If your daughter has these characteristics it is important to first work out how this has happened. It can only occur if your child has had a lot of bad experiences. Do make sure that this is not still happening. Children with a bad self-image can be helped by using the same approach as that for the difficult boy described above, but remember to keep the praise going even if it is rejected.

The *High Quality Time* is especially helpful to a child with a poor self-image, so here are some guidelines for getting the best out of this special time.

- Do something that you both enjoy, such as a game, playing outside, going for a walk, or just talking together.
- Make sure that there are no distractions, such as the TV, or disturbances, such as other people coming into the room.
- Keep this special time short and intensive so that you

both finish while you feel that you would like to do it again. Five minutes of high quality time every day or even every few days may be quite sufficient and better than many hours of ordinary time.

This special time will remind your child that she is indeed special and that what she does is important to you. In other words you are showing that you care for your child and love her, in spite of everything.

'What should I do if other children come to my house and behave badly?'

It is helpful to have very clear *house rules*. These are rules that have to be obeyed by anybody who is in your home. Don't change your rules just because you have visitors, but warn them about the rules if you think there are going to be problems. Most children will accept this arrangement

if it is made clear to them before things get too out of hand. If they still don't behave, you can always send them home early!

'My daughter claims that I am much more strict than other parents'

Most children use the example of their friends to try and get a better deal for themselves at home. There is always someone who is given more toys, more pocket money or more freedom than your poor hard-done-by child! It is worthwhile considering whether your child has a point. However, if you feel that you have got it right, there is no need for you to change. Just explain that your family has well-thought-out rules of behaviour, and that is how it is going to continue. Most children accept this quite well and even feel more secure because of it.

What if . . .

'My son is rude and swears'

Children quickly learn that being rude produces interesting reactions in other people. It is not unusual for adults to laugh at rudeness in very young children because it is so incongruous, but this only makes it more likely for the child to be rude again. Children will imitate swearing if they hear it at home or outside the home. So if you swear yourself, don't be surprised if your child does too. If you want him to stop swearing, you will first have to stop everyone in the family from swearing!

Like so many kinds of bad behaviour, rudeness is best nipped in the bud, before it becomes a habit. Here are some ideas about what you can do to achieve this:

● **Make sure that your child isn't successful in using**

rudeness or swearing to get your attention or to wind you up.

- You could try ignoring your child completely until he has said the same thing in a polite way and apologized for being rude.
- A strong and immediate overreaction to swearing can be helpful in making it quite clear that this is unacceptable. Being strong doesn't mean smacking, which should be avoided; it means being very clear indeed that rudeness is just not on. If your child still takes no notice, you obviously need a little more practice at being convincing!
- Older children (7 years +) may find it helpful to pay 5–10p for the luxury of using each swearword, with the proceeds going to a children's charity.
- It is much more difficult to control swearing outside the home, and it is therefore best to concentrate on getting it right at home so that your child knows right from wrong.

'My child has terrible tempers even though he is now 6 years old'

Tempers and bad behaviour are more common in boys than girls, but you would expect children to have a reasonable control of their temper by the time they start school at the age of 5. At 6 years of age, a temper should not last much longer than a few minutes or occur more frequently than once every few days. It is difficult to be more specific because tempers are so dependent on the circumstances in which they occur. However, if your child is still having frequent or very bad tempers after starting primary school, there must be something wrong somewhere. It may not be serious, but it needs to be dealt with. The longer a child continues to have tempers, the more serious it is and the more difficult it is to change (see *Tantrums and Tempers* in this series).

'My child steals money and other things'

Most children take things without asking at some time or another, but stealing needs to be dealt with firmly and clearly, even if your child is very young. The trouble with stealing is that it is one of the very few behaviours that is immediately rewarding. This makes it likely to happen again in spite of being found out. The most common reason for stealing is because the opportunity is there and it is possible to get away with it. So if you leave money lying around, or you collect money in a jar on the mantelpiece, don't be too surprised if it disappears. Stealing is increasingly more serious the older the child, especially after the age of 8 years old. Before you start to deal with stealing it is important to think about the possible underlying causes, as follows:

- you haven't made it clear that taking without asking is wrong
- your child has got away with stealing in the past
- you leave things lying around and make it easy for your child to steal without anyone knowing
- sometimes children take things for themselves if they are feeling miserable, jealous and/or angry
- occasionally a child will steal on the instructions of someone else, for example to pay off a bully at school
- children who find it difficult to make friends may 'buy' friendship by giving away things that they have stolen
- some children steal in a gang and may be led astray by others.

There are three important steps to take in order to deal with stealing effectively:

1. Prevention

This involves keeping money out of the child's sight and if necessary even locked up. It is only reasonable to leave money lying around if you are certain that your child doesn't steal.

2. Detection

It is important to have a system of checking so that you know if and when your child has stolen. This may mean keeping an account of the money in your bag or pocket and checking through your child's things so that you are aware of anything new that appears that can't be explained. Don't feel guilty about checking your child's personal possessions, because it is unreasonable to trust someone who is stealing.

3. Restitution

Restitution involves making things right again. So anything that has been taken has to be returned with an apology. If 10p was stolen then 10p is returned. If a toy was stolen, the toy must be returned. If something was taken but then lost or used up, the same should be returned in value or in kind. Your child should never be allowed to keep anything that has been stolen. If your child is paying back from pocket money it is best to hand over all the money and then get your child to hand back the necessary amount so that it is clear that some of the money is being taken away. It is also a good idea to leave your child with some pocket money rather than to stop it completely (see page 53).

The punishment for stealing is for your child to be found out and to know that you are upset. The apology and return of the stolen property is also part of the punishment. No further punishment should be necessary. If you do anything too tough it may make further stealing more likely out of anger and resentment.

Any child who steals should have regular pocket money so that it possible to pay back anything that has been stolen. An account book should be kept because it teaches children the value of money and where it all goes. It will also help you to be able to keep a check on what is happening with your child's money. No further pocket money should be given until you have checked that the book is up-to-date and correct.

It is also helpful for a child who steals to have a savings account where a proportion of the pocket money is saved, together with any other gifts of money. The money is saved for something special that your child particularly wants and then, if there is any further stealing, the money for paying back comes directly from the savings account. In this way the stealing is dealt with quickly.

If your child continues to steal in spite of sticking to this programme, you will have to increase the level of supervision even further. It is a good idea not to trust your child while stealing is a problem and not for six months after the last episode of stealing. It will take this long to gradually build up trust again.

Stealing outside the home can be dealt with in much the same way, but a higher level of supervision is required. It may even be necessary to accompany your child whenever he or she goes out of the house. This may seem a bit excessive, but if you are half-hearted in the way you deal with stealing, you will only be half successful!

'My child is hyperactive'

Hyperactivity is not a bad or naughty behaviour because it isn't done deliberately as can be seen from the following list of causes.

- **Hyperactivity and restlessness is a normal stage of development between the ages of 2 and 6 years. In some children, especially boys, this phase can last even longer.**
- **Distressed children who have had to cope with a lot of family stress tend to be more restless and unsettled.**
- **Children who have been allowed too much freedom to do as they please are often restless and demanding.**
- **A few children, especially those with some sort of brain disorder such as epilepsy or birth injury, are hyperactive due to a medical condition called either 'the**

hyperkinetic syndrome' or 'attention deficit disorder'.
- Children who are overstimulated and overexcited will be hyperactive.
- Lack of sleep can cause children to be overactive.
- Although there is no firm evidence, it is possible that particular foods and additives make children restless.

Hyperactive children benefit not only from dealing with the cause if possible, but also from routine and regularity in everyday life, with firm boundaries set for their behaviour. Concentration exercises can help—you could ask your child to concentrate on a task for a few seconds, timed by the clock, and then gradually increase the time over several weeks, always ending each concentration session on a note of success.

'My son is very destructive'

All children go through a destructive phase at some time or another, but there are several possible causes for destructive behaviour:

- On the whole boys are more often destructive than girls.
- Some children (especially boys) are more clumsy by nature and therefore more likely to break things accidentally. It is no good getting cross and upset if this is the case because it won't help and it may even make things worse. Clumsy children need extra supervision and practice at being careful, together with praise when they get it right.
- Younger children are naturally more clumsy and destructive, so it is unfair to give them rather delicate or sophisticated toys to play with and then get upset when the toys are damaged.
- Sometimes children will be deliberately destructive if they are angry or jealous, but if this is the case the

choice of target will be obvious. The best method of dealing with this is to get the child to replace whatever has been damaged and give an apology. If the cost is high then money can be earned by doing extra jobs around the house.

- Children with a poor self-image sometimes go out of their way to be destructive and deliberately damage things. It is important to recognize this cause of destructive behaviour, because nothing will make things better unless the child's self-image is improved (see page 65).

- Distressed children who live in a disorganized, unpredictable and insecure environment are often destructive in a particular way. They tend to tear up their clothes, bed clothes and wallpaper. They mix things together and make a mess and they may even be destructive to themselves. It is a worrying sign if these behaviours continue and it indicates that a radical rethink is necessary about how things are organized at home.

It is important to distinguish between accidental damage which requires no punishment and deliberate destructiveness, where some form of restitution is necessary. In other words, try and make the punishment fit the crime.

'My daughter tells lies'

Like the understanding of right and wrong, the concept of lying only develops gradually and is not well established until 8–10 years of age. Younger children need to be taught that it is wrong to tell lies, but older children require some form of discipline for lying. The most effective form of punishment is for your child to be found out and for you to be upset and disappointed.

It is important to develop the skill of detecting when your child is lying so that she doesn't get away with it, because this is the most common reason for lying. Some children are more difficult to 'read' than others, but every child will have some tell-tale sign which will give them away; it is just a question of knowing what it is.

If your child has got stuck in the habit of telling lies, think about the following questions:

- Why hasn't your child learnt that it is wrong to lie? Has she been slow learning other things as well?
- Can your child tell lies and get away with it?
- Does your child steal as well, because stealing and lying often go hand in hand?
- What has your child got to hide? Is she afraid of your reaction to the truth?
- Do you trust your child too much?
- Has your child got some other reason to tell lies, such as wanting people to believe that she is a better person than she is in reality?

If your child regularly tells lies, it is best not to believe what she says until you have checked for yourself that the story is correct. Children who lie should know that they are not believed and that trust can only be built up by telling the truth.

'My son lights fires'

Fire setting is obviously dangerous and should never be allowed to happen at all. This means training your child right from the beginning about the dangers of fire. If, in spite of your training, your child lights a fire without your permission, your reaction should be so memorable that it never happens again. It isn't unusual for children between the ages of 4 and 6 years old to experiment with fire, without knowing how dangerous it is. So at these ages it is particularly important to keep matches and fires well away and to give a high level of supervision and training.

Children who repeatedly set fires have one or more of the following problems:

- the child is poorly supervised
- there are problems in the relationships at home which have caused the child to be distressed and to want to draw attention to himself
- insufficient training about the danger of fire has been given
- the fire setting is part of a wider behaviour problem and indicates serious disturbance
- lighting fires may have become something of a habit, a way of having excitement from watching the fire and everyone's reactions to it, especially if the fire brigade is called.

Children who set fires over the age of 6 years old are a particular cause for concern. A very high level of care and supervision is needed.

'My daughter behaves badly in a sexual way'

Children will copy the sexual behaviour that they see around them, and will generally adopt the standards that their parents set. However, the TV and videos can also be very influential. Adult sexual behaviour is clearly inappropriate in a child, so it is important to keep this side of your life to yourself. At the same time it is important to teach your child what sort of sexual behaviour is acceptable at the different stages of development.

If your child behaves in an inappropriately sexual way, you should consider the following possibilities:

- Has adult sexual behaviour or talk been witnessed at home?
- Has your child seen adult sex on the TV or video?
- Has your child picked up ideas from other children?
- Could she have seen pornographic magazines?

- **Is it possible that there has been some form of sexual abuse?**

Each cause has a fairly obvious solution, but if you believe that your child has been sexually abused it will be necessary to seek expert help.

'My son plays truant from school'

Playing truant can be distinguished from school phobia because in the latter case the parents know where the child is, but with truancy neither the parents nor the teachers know where the child is. As a general rule, children who play truant on their own are more disturbed than when it is done in a group. However, all truancy should be a cause for concern, particularly if it is from primary school.

There are several possible reasons why children hop off school:

- **The school is boring or difficult for the child and seems to have nothing much to offer.**
- **Your son is being led astray by other children (why is your child so easily led?)**
- **The school is disorganized and doesn't check up on truancy.**
- **Truancy may occur where the parents are preoccupied with other problems, such as marital difficulties or both parents working.**
- **If your son has other antisocial behaviour as well as truancy, it probably means that he has quite serious problems and is out of your control. Perhaps you need some specialist outside help.**
- **Maybe your son isn't getting enough supervision. Communication between home and school needs to be tightened up, perhaps with the help of a daily diary that goes between home and school.**

- Sometimes children play truant because they have found something much more interesting to do, such as a paid job or meeting a friend.

As soon as you find out that your child is playing truant, it is important to work out which of the various factors are causing the problem and to have a meeting with the school. It helps to have a system worked out with the school where they agree to contact you if your child doesn't turn up. It may even be necessary to keep a check at every lesson and for the child to stay with a teacher at break times.

'My daughter keeps bad company and is easily led'

Peer group pressure is a powerful force to reckon with, but even in adolescence most children will follow their parents' views when it comes to the crunch. Some parents feel that they have no right to interfere with their children's friendships, but equally parents have a right and indeed a duty to protect children from being led astray. It is therefore entirely reasonable for you to be quite intrusive and if necessary intervene in a potentially damaging relationship. Obviously this is a delicate area and you will need to be careful but not over-sensitive about it.

'My son sniffs glue'

Glue sniffing and abuse of other substances is extremely dangerous and worrying. It indicates that there is something wrong if it happens more than once and it is better to see the problem as having more to do with failure and distress than with bad behaviour. The following failures are commonly associated with substance abuse:

- unsatisfactory relationships at home and outside

- academic failure at school
- a breakdown in communication at home and/or between home and school
- a failure to supervise adequately
- low self-esteem and a feeling of failure.

The underlying causes need to be dealt with, together
with the provision of a high level of supervision and loving
care. The problem is complicated, however, and outside
help is frequently required.

'My children argue and answer back all the time'

It is always difficult to get the balance right between
allowing children freedom to speak their mind and not
letting them be opinionated and bloody-minded. If you
feel that the balance is not quite right with your children
and your friends agree with you, then you will have to do
some determined work and take a tough stand in order to
get any change. Children easily get stuck in the habit of
arguing and answering back so that it happens automatically without the child realizing it. If you want to break the
habit, it is no good being subtle or half-hearted—you will
have to go for it in a big way!

'My child is aggressive and fights a lot'

Fighting and agression are not unusual in young children
and a lot will depend on what standards of behaviour you
set. If marked aggressive behaviour continues much after
starting at school, then there are likely to be serious
consequences. (See *Fighting, Teasing and Bullying* in this
series.)

APPENDIX 1

WHAT THE RESEARCH SHOWS

Difficult and disruptive behaviour has been extensively studied and there is now good agreement on the main facts which I will outline here. I hope that you will be able to use this information when you are wondering why your child seems to be naughty and whether other children are just as badly behaved. Several different terms are used for bad behaviour which has got out of hand and is causing distress, such as *conduct disorder, behaviour disorder, antisocial or deviant behaviour*, but they all refer to behaviours that are outside the range that parents normally regard as acceptable.

Surveys

Naomi Richman and her colleagues conducted a survey of 3-year-old children in Walthamstow, London, and found that 7 per cent had moderate or severe behaviour problems (Richman et al., 1982). The British Birth Survey followed up all children born in one week in April 1970 and found that at 5 years of age approximately 10 per cent of children were reported to be often disobedient and 'quick to fly off the handle' (Golding and Rush, 1986). A survey of children aged 7 years old in New Zealand found that 20 per cent showed some form of antisocial behaviour such as destructiveness or disobedience, with or without hyperactivity, and 9 per cent had behaviour problems that persisted

(McGee et al., 1984). Although these studies might seem to show that bad behaviour increases with age, this is more likely to be due to a parent's changing perception of what is unacceptable at different ages and the fact that larger children can make more of an impact!

A very important survey of children aged 10–11 years of age living in the Isle of Wight was carried out by Professor Michael Rutter and others. They used parent and teacher observations together with detailed interviews of the children. About 25 per cent of the children were noted to be disobedient at home, but at school less than 10 per cent were disobedient; 4 per cent of the children were found to have a serious behaviour problem that was severe enough to be a handicap. As in most other surveys of naughty children, more boys than girls were reported to have bad behaviour (Rutter et al., 1970).

Difficult behaviour and temperament

Alexander Thomas and Stella Chess (1977) carried out a classic study of a group of children in New York. They looked at nine temperamental characteristics and noted that the following were associated with an increased frequency of difficult behaviour, including tempers and irritability:

- irregular, unpredictable eating and sleeping habits
- strong, mostly negative moods
- slow to adapt to new situations.

Similar findings were reported by Professor Philip Graham et al. (1973) in London. They identified a temperamental adversity index, using the above characteristics. The index was able to predict those children who were likely to have problems a year later. A high score gave a three-fold increase in the risk of difficult behaviour at home and an eight-fold risk of problems at school. Children who show the above characteristics from birth onwards are often said to have 'the difficult child syndrome'.

The influence of the family

Patterson (1982) has described antisocial behaviours in children and aggressive behaviours in parents which lead on to a predictable sequence of events called 'the coercive system' as follows:

1. Badly behaved children make it difficult for their parents to use the more subtle forms of management of deviant behaviour and to encourage good behaviour.
2. The naughty child frequently produces an aggressive response from the parent, which then serves as a model or example for the child to follow. Alternatively the parent may give in 'for a quiet life', in which case the child will learn that it pays to be bad.
3. The level of disturbance and aggression in the family rises and anarchy follows, leading to a further breakdown of caring and positive, helping behaviours in family interactions.
4. As a result, the parents tend to become fed up and irritable. They lose their confidence and self-esteem and their children also become frustrated and fed up.
5. Family members disengage from each other, the parents become disunited and the control of antisocial behaviour breaks down, resulting in still further problems—and so the cycle continues.

The association of various family factors with antisocial behaviour has been reviewed by Sula Wolff. She found that the following factors were statistically linked to conduct disorder (Wolff, 1985):

• absence of the father
• loss of a parent through divorce rather than through death

- a depressed mother
- an irritable parent
- marital discord
- socioeconomic disadvantage
- large family size.

Each of these factors could be the cause or the result of the badly behaved child and it is difficult to tell which comes first. For example, having a difficult child would be enough to make any parent irritable, but on the other hand it is easy to see how an irritable and hostile parent could make a child feel angry and frustrated. What usually happens is that a vicious cycle develops between the child and the parent, each making the other more hostile and upset. The immediate effect of these influences is more obvious in boys, but there is some evidence that girls may show more adverse effects in the long term (Rutter, 1982).

Other factors

Although family factors play a part in the development of bad behaviour, other causes have also been identified (McGee et al., 1984, Barron and Earls, 1984, 1985):

- babies who are smaller than expected size for their gestational age
- brain damage, whatever the cause
- poor verbal ability
- specific reading delay
- hearing difficulty
- two or more changes of school in the first two years
- stressful life events
- poor housing.

Bad behaviour therefore has highly complex relationships with a wide range of family and social influences. To some extent the child plays only a small part in the generation of problem behaviours and yet it is the child who normally takes most of the blame!

Behaviour problems at school

Bad behaviour also occurs in a school context, where it has been shown that the most frequent reason for suspension is aggressive behaviour (Nicol et al., 1985). Boys are more likely to be excluded from school than girls and once excluded, very few children return to normal schooling (Galloway et al., 1982).

Children with specific reading problems have consistently been found to fail at school and to have a higher frequency of behaviour problems when compared with children who have no difficulty with reading. Most studies suggest that there is a highly complex relationship between the bad behaviour and the reading problem, with both having some causative factors in common (Rutter and Madge, 1976).

The school itself may have characteristics which encourage or at least allow the development of antisocial behaviour (Reynolds and Sullivan, 1981). Several studies show that even if school intake factors are allowed for, there remain consistent differences between schools in the rate of antisocial behaviour seen in the children. The most likely explanation for these differences is that they have been caused by the school. They include the following factors:

- low staff morale
- high teacher turnover
- unclear standards of behaviour
- inconsistent methods of discipline
- poor organization
- lack of awareness of children as individuals.

What happens to children with anti-social behaviour?

The sociologist Lee Robins (1978) carried out important long-term studies of antisocial children in America and found that some 90 per cent of antisocial adults engaged in similar behaviour as children. This worrying finding is balanced by the finding that about half of the antisocial children did not grow up into sociopathic adults and this type of behaviour in preschool children does not usually lead to similar problems later on.

It does seem however, that from school age onwards antisocial behaviour has a strong tendency to continue as a very stable characteristic which may be difficult to change (Olweus, 1979). Philip Graham and Michael Rutter (1973) studied secondary school children and found that over a period of three years, 50 per cent of the children with bad behaviour continued to cause problems.

The following factors have been found to be associated with a poor outcome for antisocial behaviour in children (Kelso and Stewart, 1986):

- frequent bad behaviour
- aggressive, argumentative and disruptive
- fire setting
- mixing with other antisocial children
- truancy and lying
- growing up in extreme poverty
- misuse of drugs
- running off
- early onset of problems
- a wide range of behaviour problems
- other members of the family who show antisocial behaviour
- a history of alcohol problems in the family.

Conclusions

The research findings suggest that as children grow older there is a strong tendency for bad behaviour to persist, even into adult life. Family influences interact with the child's characteristics in such a way that the child is predisposed to develop antisocial activities. This in turn leads to rejection and isolation of the child by others, resulting in a deep sense of anger and frustration and further bad behaviour. Eventually, as the child grows older, a poor self-image is formed and a strong feeling of failure which fuels the vicious cycle. This pessimistic outlook need not happen if the factors leading to problem behaviours are understood, and something is done about it early on while the child is still young.

APPENDIX 2

HELP!

What to do when all else fails

Almost every parent has the experience of trying everything to get their child to behave and yet nothing seems to work. Just in case this happens to you, here is a check-list for you to go through to remind you of the more important things to consider when you are wondering what on earth to do next.

The common causes for discipline not working

- Does your child really believe that you mean what you say?
- Is your discipline often inconsistent?
- Perhaps your child doesn't know what standard of behaviour you expect?
- Have you given enough praise for good behaviour?
- Could your child be copying the bad behaviour of others in the family?
- Have you given up too quickly or too easily, just for a quiet life?
- Perhaps the bad behaviour has become stuck as a habit and happens automatically without your child even thinking?

- Maybe you aren't that serious about discipline, or you have something else on your mind?
- Are you giving enough time and supervision to your child?
- Have you lost your sense of humour?
- Could the timing of your discipline be too late or too slow to be effective?
- Do you think that your discipline could have been undermined by someone close to your child?
- Perhaps you have a child with a difficult temperament?
- Is it possible that your child has developed a poor self-image and behaves badly because he or she feels bad?
- Have you considered the possibility that your child could be upset or unsettled by problems at home or at school?
- Could your child be suffering from some kind of illness or are you unwell yourself?

As a rough guide I have listed the causes in order of frequency, with the most frequent cause first. Usually there will be several different causes for your discipline not working, each interacting with the other factors to make it quite difficult to tell what is going on and impossible to find *the* cause for the bad behaviour.

Some ideas for what to do if your discipline doesn't work

In some cases just knowing the cause or causes will be enough to show you what has to be done to put things right, but if you are still stuck, here are some ideas to get you unstuck:

- Remember to use the 6 Cs of good discipline—Constantly Communicate Clearly with Consistency, Conviction and Care.

- Do try to use praise and encouragement and avoid hostile rejection and criticism.
- Have you really tried all of the approaches described in this book and tried each method of discipline for at least six weeks?
- Here is a mnemonic to help you remember what to do

P	Persist and don't give in
R	Respond immediately
A	Always be consistent
I	Ignore silly behaviour and praise the good
S	Say your bit—and that should be it!
E	Expect the best always

If you have done all this and you are still stuck, then how about trying the following:

- Ask three good friends for their opinion, but only take notice of what they say if they all agree on what you should do.
- Have a *very* serious talk with your child and the rest of the family all together to explain about the importance of getting on with each other in the family.
- Get everyone together who knows your child well and pool your ideas to agree a plan of action.
- Read the book again!

If things have still not improved at least you know that you have done everything, so please don't feel guilty—it only makes things worse. How about taking a break, you probably need a change and a rest by now! There is bound to be someone somewhere who can help you out and look after your child while you have some time for yourself. Finally, I hope you remember those strong feelings of love and joy that you have for your child. It is important to hold on to these positive and creative emotions when the going is tough. They will help to carry you through and protect both you and your child from harmful rejection and hostile criticism.

It is always difficult to know when is the right time to get professional help with a family problem, and even more difficult to know where to go and whom to ask. Here are some suggestions if you feel it is necessary to get some outside help:

- Ask other parents and professionals what they know of the local services, but take what they say with a pinch of salt, because individual opinions may be unreliable. One of the best-informed people is likely to be your GP.
- Voluntary groups for parents can be very supportive and give you an idea of how other people have coped. They don't give professional advice, but they should be able to advise on how to get this type of help.
- There is a wide range of professional groups who have specialized training and experience with children's emotional and behavioural problems. The difference between the various professions is confusing to say the least. One way round this problem is to ask your GP to refer you to the local Child Psychiatry Service where it is usual for a range of different professions to work closely together.
- Don't be put off by a referral to a Consultant Child Psychiatrist; they are medically-qualified doctors with a very broad training in the full range of children's problems. They have special skills in helping any problem of emotions or behaviour which seems to be getting out of control and out of proportion to what might be expected, given the circumstances.

REFERENCES

Barron, A. P., Earls, F., The relation of temperament and social factors to behaviour problems in three year old children, (1984) J. Child Psychol. Psychiat., 25, 23-33.

Galloway, D. M., Ball, T., Blomfield, D., Boyd, R. *Schools and Disruptive Pupils*, Longman, London (1982).

Golding, J., Rush, D., Temper tantrums and other behaviour problems, in: *From Birth to Five*, N. R. Butler & J. Golding (eds) Pergamon Press, Oxford (1986).

Graham, P., Rutter, M. Psychiatric disorder in the young adolescent: a follow up study, (1973) Proc. Royal Soc. Medicine, 66, 1226-29.

Graham, P., Rutter, M., George, S., Temperamental Characteristics as predictors of behaviour problems in children, (1973) Amer. J. Orthopsychiat., 43, 328-39.

Kelso, J., Stewart, M. A., Factors which predict the persistence of aggressive conduct disorder, (1986). J. Child Psychol. Psychiat., 27, 77-86.

McGee, R., Williams, S., Silva, P. A., Behavioural and developmental characteristics of aggressive, hyperactive and aggressive-hyperactive boys, (1984). J. Amer. Acad. Child Psychiat., 23, 270-279.

Nicol, A. R., Willcox, C., Hibbert, K. What sort of children are suspended from school and what can we do for them?

(1985) in: *Longitudinal Studies in Child Psychology and Psychiatry* A. R. Nicol (ed.) Wiley, Chichester.

Olweus, D., Stability of aggressive reaction patterns in males: a review, (1979). Psychological Bulletin, 86, 852-875.

Patterson, G. R., *Coersive Family Process*. Castelia Publishing, Oregon (1982).

Reynolds, D., Sullivan, M., The effects of school: A radical faith restated, (1981) in: *Problem Behaviour in the Secondary School*, B. Gillam (ed.) Croom Helm, London.

Richman, N., Behaviour problems in preschool children: family and social factors, (1977). Brit. J. Psychiatry., 131, 523-527.

Richman, N., Stevenson, J., Graham, P., (1982). *Preschool to School: a Behavioural study*. Academic Press, London.

Robins, L. N. Sturdy childhood predictors of adult anti-social behaviour: replications from longitudinal studies, (1978). Psychological Medicine, 8, 611-622.

Rutter, M., Epidemiological-longitudinal approaches to the study of development (1982), in: *The Concept of Development*, Vol 15, W. A. Collins (ed.) Lawrence Erlbaum, New Jersey.

Rutter, M., Madge, N., *Cycles of Disadvantage*. Heinemann, London (1976).

Rutter, M., Tizard, J., Whitmore, K. (eds.) *Education, Health and Behaviour*. Longman, London (1970).

Thomas, A., Chess, S., *Temperament and Development*. Brunner/Mazel, New York (1977).

Wolff, S., Non-delinquent disturbance of conduct, (1985) in: *Child and Adolescent Psychiatry: Modern Approaches*, M. Rutter and L. Hersov (eds.) Blackwell Scientific, Oxford.

FURTHER READING

Scientific Foundations of Developmental Psychiatry.
Edited by Michael Rutter. Published by Heinemann Medical Books, London. (1980)
An excellent reference book on the wider aspects of child development.

Conduct Disorders of Childhood and Adolescence: A social learning Perspective
By Martin Herbert. Published by John Wiley, Chichester. (1987 2nd ed)
A very detailed and technical book.

Temperamental Differences in Infants and Young Children.
Ciba Foundation Symposium 89. Published by Pitman, London. (1982)
A helpful collection of papers presented at a symposium of world authorities on temperament.

Behaviour Problems in Childhood: A Primary Care Approach.
Edited by Stewart Gabel. Published by Grune & Stratton, New York
A wide ranging American medical text book.

Behavioural Treatment of Problem Children: A Practice Manual.
By Martin Herbert. Published by Academic Press, London and Grune & Stratton, New York (1981)
A highly technical book on behaviour therapy.

INDEX